Homemade Treats
for Your
Furry Friends

Olivia Willson

MJ&D Publishing
P.O. Box 11193
Spring Hill, FL 34610
http://www.mjdpublishing.com

ASIN: BOOPQYUNVQ

DISCLAIMER

CONTENTS

INTRODUCTION

We enjoy giving treats to our pets almost as much as they enjoy eating them. When used in moderation, giving treats adds an extra positive dimension to our relationship with our dogs and cats. We use treats to reward good behavior, to strengthen the bond that we share with our pets, and—let's face it—just because we love them!

With pet owners becoming increasingly concerned about the ingredients in commercially prepared pet treats, making them at home is a great way to ensure that you know exactly what your dogs and cats are eating. Homemade treats also make great gifts to give your friends' and family's pets, especially at holiday time.

Making pet treats is surprisingly easy. It's also a great activity to share with children!

Because most of the recipes are fast and easy to make, the little ones won't get bored and impatient as quickly as they do with other cooking projects. With a variety of recipes to try and choose from, this book is sure to provide some new favorites that your pets will love.

Food for thought:

These recipes are for treats, not a replacement for pet food. Dogs and cats have specific nutritional requirements not duplicated in treats.

🐾 Because these treats are homemade, they do not contain certain preservatives present in some commercially prepared treats. Most of them should be consumed within a week of making them (not that this should be a problem!), and some should be refrigerated after preparation. If a recipe ingredient should normally be refrigerated (meat, eggs, milk), please store the treats in the refrigerator in an airtight container.

🐾 Certain foods should never be given to pets. Some human foods (onions, for example) are unsafe for pets and can even be toxic. Do not add extra ingredients to these recipes with potentially unsafe foods.

Human food can be toxic to pets in frequent or large doses (like tuna for cats) so use caution.

🐾 Some pets have food sensitivities and allergies. If you are making pet treats for your friends or relatives, please check with them first before giving them as gifts.

Enjoy making treats for your dogs and cats with ingredients that you can recognize and pronounce. Your furry friends will thank you!

1 Cat Treats

CAT TREATS: Tuna Crunchies

1 small can or pouch of tuna in water, drained
1 cup wheat flour
1 egg
1 tablespoon vegetable oil
1 teaspoon dried catnip (optional)

Preheat oven to 350°F.

Combine tuna, flour, egg, olive oil and catnip (optional). Mix until smooth.

Roll dough into treat-sized balls and place on a cookie sheet lined with parchment paper. Flatten treats slightly with the back of a fork.

Bake 10 to 12 minutes until lightly browned. Remove from oven and place pan on cooling rack.

Store treats in an airtight container in the refrigerator for up to a week.

CAT TREATS: No-Bake Sardine Delights

2 cans sardines in oil, undrained
2/3 cup cooked white rice (no seasonings)
1 tablespoon liver or meat baby food (no onion, onion powder or garlic)

Mash sardines and baby food. Add rice and mix thoroughly.

Divide into treat-sized balls.

Store treats in an airtight container in refrigerator for up to two days.

CAT TREATS: Turkey Mini Meatballs

1/2 pound ground turkey
1/2 cup plain bread crumbs
1/4 cup grated cheddar or parmesan cheese
1/4 cup powdered milk
1 tablespoon brewer's yeast
1 large egg

Preheat oven to 350°F.

Thoroughly combine all ingredients in a large bowl.

Roll the mixture into 1-2-inch balls and place on a nonstick cookie sheet.

Bake for approximately 20 minutes until meatballs reach an internal temperature of 160°F. Remove from oven and allow it to cool.

Store cooked treats in refrigerator for up to two days. Freeze any cooked treats that will not be consumed within two days and defrost before serving.

CAT TREATS: Mackerel Crunch

1/2 cup canned mackerel, mashed
1 cup plain bread crumbs
1 tablespoon vegetable oil
1 egg, lightly beaten

Preheat oven to 350°F.

Mix together all ingredients thoroughly.

Roll the mixture into 1-inch balls and place on a lightly greased baking sheet.

Bake for 7-8 minutes. Remove from oven and allow it to cool.

Store cooked treats in an airtight container in the refrigerator.

CAT TREATS: Crunchy Salmon Bites

1 small can of salmon
1/2 cup cornmeal
1/4 cup powdered milk
1 egg
1 tablespoon vegetable oil
2 tablespoons low sodium chicken broth or water
1 cup wheat flour

Preheat oven to 350°F.

Mix salmon, cornmeal, powdered milk, egg, vegetable oil and broth.

Add flour to mixture, kneading by hand, until mixed well.

Put dough ball on a lightly floured surface and roll to ¼-inch thickness with a flour coated rolling pin.

Cut into treat-sized pieces and put treats on a nonstick baking sheet.

Bake for 12-15 minutes. Remove from oven and allow it to cool.

Store treats in an airtight container in the refrigerator.

CAT TREATS: Crunchy Chicken Bites

1-½ cups cooked chicken, shredded fine
1/3 cup cornmeal
1/2 cup low sodium chicken broth
1 tablespoon butter, softened
1 cup wheat flour

Preheat oven to 350°F.

Mix together the chicken, cornmeal, broth and butter.

Add flour to mixture, kneading by hand, until mixed well.

Put dough ball on a lightly floured surface and roll to ¼-inch thickness with a flour coated rolling pin.

Cut into treat-sized pieces and put treats on a nonstick baking sheet.

Bake for approximately 20 minutes. Remove from oven and allow it to cool.

Store treats in an airtight container in the refrigerator.

CAT TREATS: Chicken Liver Snacks

1/2 cup cooked chicken livers
1-¼ cup wheat flour
1/4 cup low sodium chicken broth
1 tablespoon butter, softened

Preheat oven to 325°F.

Mix chicken livers and chicken broth in blender.

Combine chicken liver mix, flour and butter.

Roll dough into treat-sized balls and place on a greased cookie sheet. Flatten treats slightly with the back of a fork.

Bake for 10 to 12 minutes. Remove from oven and allow it to cool. Store treats in an airtight container in the refrigerator.

CAT TREATS: Tuna and Egg Surprise

1 can of tuna (6 oz)
Juice from tuna can plus enough water to make 1/4 cup liquid
1/2 cup wheat flour
1/4 cup cornmeal
4 tablespoons chopped cooked egg white

Preheat oven to 350°F.

Mix tuna, tuna juice, cornmeal and egg.

Add flour to mixture, kneading by hand, until mixed well.

Put dough ball on a lightly floured surface and roll to ¼-inch thickness with a flour coated rolling pin.

Cut into treat-sized pieces and put treats on a nonstick baking sheet. Bake for approximately 20 minutes. Remove from oven and allow it to cool.

Store treats in an airtight container in the refrigerator.

CAT TREATS: Cheese Munchies

3/4 cup grated cheddar cheese
3/4 cup wheat flour
1/4 cup corn meal
1/4 cup sour cream

Preheat oven to 350°F.

Mix together cheese, sour cream and cornmeal.

Add flour to mixture, kneading by hand, until mixed well.

Put dough ball on a lightly floured surface and roll to ¼-inch thickness with a flour coated rolling pin.

Cut into treat-sized pieces and put treats on a greased baking sheet.

Bake for 20-25 minutes. Remove from oven and allow it to cool.

Store treats in an airtight container in the refrigerator.

CAT TREATS: Turkey Cheese Patties

4 oz ground turkey
4 tablespoons plain bread crumbs
1 tablespoon condensed cream of chicken soup
1 egg
1/2 cup grated cheddar cheese

Combine turkey, bread crumbs, soup and egg.

Form mixture into several small patties and fry or broil until done.

Top patties with cheese and place them under the broiler until cheese is melted.

Cool before serving; refrigerate unused portions.

CAT TREATS: Irresistible Cheesy Snacks

1/2 cup grated cheddar cheese
1/2 cup wheat flour
2 tablespoons unsalted butter, softened
1 uncooked egg white
1/8 teaspoon dried catnip (optional)

Preheat oven to 300°F.

Stir catnip into flour (optional).

Combine cheese, butter and egg white. Add flour to cheese mixture and mix well.

Roll dough into treat-sized balls and place on a nonstick baking sheet. Flatten treats slightly with the back of a fork.

Bake 20-25 minutes. Remove from oven and allow it to cool.

Store cooked treats in an airtight container in the refrigerator.

CAT TREATS: Microwave Mini Bites

3 jars of meat baby food (without onion, onion powder or garlic ingredients)
1-½ cups wheat germ
1 teaspoon low sodium chicken broth

Combine the ingredients. Place treat-sized spoonfuls on a microwave-safe plate and cover.

Microwave the plate on high power 4-8 minutes until treats are firm but not hard.

Store treats in an airtight container in the refrigerator.

2 DOG TREATS

DOG TREATS: Frosty Fruit Drops

1 large banana
1/4 cup of blueberries or chopped strawberries

Blend banana and berries in blender until mashed but still firm. Or mash by hand.

Place treat-sized balls onto a plate lined with waxed paper.

Put treats on plate in freezer for 5-6 hours until frozen.

Store frozen treats in an airtight container in freezer.

For a pretty color variety, make one batch with blueberries and one batch with strawberries.

DOG TREATS: Cheesy Bacon and Eggs

8 medium eggs
4 slices cooked bacon, crumbled
2-¼ cups grated cheddar cheese
1 cup milk
1 tablespoon plus one teaspoon parsley

Preheat oven to 325°F.

Grease 2 muffin tins thoroughly and set aside.

With a fork, mix the eggs and milk. Stir in parsley.

Add bacon and cheese to the egg mixture and mix well.

Pour into muffin tins, filling each cup about halfway.

Bake approximately 30 minutes, until set in the center. Remove from oven and gently remove treats from tins. Cool before serving.

Store leftover treats in refrigerator.

DOG TREATS: Cookie Cutter Biscuits

2-½ cups wheat flour
3/4 cup water
1/2 cup peanut butter
2 teaspoons baking powder
4 pieces of cooked bacon, crumbled (save the grease)
Grease from the cooked bacon
1 egg

Preheat oven to 325°F.

Thoroughly combine the flour and baking powder. Add crumbled bacon.

Soften the peanut butter (this can be done, carefully, in the microwave).

In a separate bowl, combine softened peanut butter, water, bacon grease and egg.

Add peanut butter mixture to flour mixture and stir well. Knead until dough ball forms.

Put dough ball on a lightly floured surface and roll to ½-inch thickness with a flour coated rolling pin.

Cut desired shapes with cookie cutter and put treats on a greased cookie sheet.

Bake approximately 15 minutes. Remove from oven and place pan on cooling rack. Store treats in an airtight container in the refrigerator or freezer.

DOG TREATS: Bacon and Cheese Delights

2-¾ cups wheat flour
1/2 teaspoon baking powder
1/4 teaspoon baking soda
8 slices cooked bacon, crumbled
3/4 cup shredded cheddar cheese
1 teaspoon vegetable oil
1 cup water

Preheat oven to 350°F.

Thoroughly combine the flour, baking powder and baking soda.

Add bacon, cheese, vegetable oil and water to the flour mixture. Knead until dough ball forms.

Roll into 2-inch balls (smaller for small dog treats) and flatten slightly. Make a round dent in center of treat balls.

Place balls on a cookie sheet lined with parchment paper.

Bake 40-45 minutes or until treats are very lightly browned. Remove from oven and allow it to cool.

Store treats in an airtight container in the refrigerator.

These treats become very hard if overcooked, so watch baking time carefully.

DOG TREATS: Chicken Biscuits

2-½ cups wheat flour
1/2 cup powdered milk
1/4 cup canned chicken
1 medium egg
1/4 cup chicken broth (more if needed)

Preheat oven to 350°F.

Thoroughly combine flour and powdered milk.

Lightly whisk egg. Add chicken and broth to egg and mix well.

Add flour mixture to chicken and egg mixture and knead until firm dough ball forms. Add additional broth (or water) if needed.

Put dough ball on a lightly floured surface and roll to ¼-inch thickness with a flour coated rolling pin.

Cut into desired shapes with cookie cutter and put treats on greased baking sheet.

Bake for 30 minutes. Remove from oven and allow it to cool.

Store treats in an airtight container in the refrigerator.

DOG TREATS: Apple Cinnamon Biscuits

4-½ cups wheat flour or brown rice flour
1/2 cup powdered milk
1/2 teaspoon cinnamon
1 cup unsweetened applesauce
1/2 cup vegetable oil
1 cup water
2 eggs, beaten

Preheat oven to 350°F.

Combine flour, powdered milk and cinnamon.

In a separate bowl, mix together applesauce, oil, water and eggs.

Add flour mixture to applesauce mixture and knead until dough ball forms.

Put dough ball on a lightly floured surface and roll to ¼–½-inch thickness with a flour-coated rolling pin.

Cut into desired shapes with cookie cutter and put treats on greased baking sheet.

Bake for approximately 20 minutes. Remove from oven and allow it to cool.

Store treats in an airtight container in the refrigerator.

DOG TREATS: Easy Sweet Potato Treats

2-½ cups wheat flour
1 medium sweet potato, cooked and mashed (skins removed)
1/4 cup natural applesauce (unsweetened)
2 medium eggs

Preheat oven to 350°F.

Combine flour, applesauce and eggs. Add mashed sweet potato and mix well.

Place dough onto a floured surface and flatten to ¼–½-inch thickness.

Cut dough into strips or desired shapes and put treats on a nonstick baking sheet.

Bake for 35 minutes (40 minutes for crisper treats). Remove from oven and allow it to cool.

Store treats in an airtight container. Refrigerate leftover treats.

DOG TREATS: Easy Sweet Potato Treats

1 sweet potato

Preheat oven to 300°F.

Slice sweet potato lengthwise into ¼-inch strips. Place strips on greased baking sheet.

Bake for 25-30 minutes; turn over and bake another 25-30 minutes. Remove from oven and allow it to cool.

Store treats in an airtight container.

DOG TREATS: Banana Munchies

3 cups oatmeal
1 cup wheat flour
1/2 cup low fat milk
1/4 cup vegetable oil
5 tablespoons honey
2 bananas, mashed
1 large egg

Preheat oven to 325°F.

Thoroughly combine oatmeal and flour.

In a separate bowl, mix together egg, milk, oil, honey and mashed bananas.

Add the flour mixture to the banana mixture and stir well.

Pour batter onto a greased baking pan or greased metal brownie pans.

Bake for 20-25 minutes. Remove from oven and allow it to cool. When cool, cut into treat-sized pieces.

Store treats in an airtight container in the refrigerator.

DOG TREATS: Frozen Yummy Pops

4 cups lowfat plain yogurt
3/4 cup blueberries or chopped strawberries
1 banana, mashed
4 tablespoons creamy peanut butter
1/2 teaspoon vanilla extract

Combine all ingredients and mix well.

Blend the mixture in a blender until the consistency of a smoothie.

Pour mix into ice cube trays and freeze.

Store treats, covered, in the freezer for up to 4 months.

DOG TREATS: Cheese Lover Biscuits

1 cup wheat flour
1/2 cup shredded cheddar cheese
1/4 cup grated Romano cheese
1/2 cup evaporated milk
1/2 teaspoon parsley
1 large egg

Preheat oven to 350°F.

Combine ingredients and mix thoroughly.

Roll dough into treat-sized balls and place them on a greased cookie sheet.

Bake for 10-12 minutes. Remove from oven and allow it to cool.

Store treats in an airtight container in the refrigerator.

DOG TREATS: Salmon Delights

1 large can salmon, undrained
2 cups wheat flour
2 medium eggs, lightly beaten

Preheat oven to 350°F.

Combine eggs and salmon. Slowly add flour and mix well.

Turn out dough onto a floured surface and flatten to ¼-inch thickness.

Place flattened dough on a greased baking pan.

Bake for 25 minutes (30 minutes for crispier treats). Remove from oven and immediately remove dough from pan. Allow to cool.

Cut into treat-sized pieces.

Store treats in an airtight container in the refrigerator or freezer.

DOG TREATS: Microwave Minis

4 jars meat baby food (no onion, onion powder or garlic ingredients)
1-½ cup wheat germ
1 teaspoon low sodium chicken broth

Combine ingredients. If mixture is too soft, add a small additional amount of flour or wheat germ.

 Place treat-sized spoonfuls on a microwave-safe plate and cover.

Microwave the treats on high power 5-7 minutes until firm but not hard.

Store treats in an airtight container in the refrigerator.

Made in United States
Troutdale, OR
03/28/2025

30079463R00021